ISSUES In The HEART

Master Them

The

Collaboration of Litigation Strategy
and God's Law

LUCINDA JONES, Esq.

Issues In The Heart
An Advocate Lucinda Publication
P.O. Box 442111
Detroit, Michigan 48244

This guide or parts thereof may not be reproduced in any form, stored in a retrieval system, or transmitted in any form by any means -- electronic, mechanical, photocopy, recording, or otherwise -- without prior written permission of the publisher, except as provided by the United States of America copyright law.

All Scripture quotations are from the King James Version of the Bible.

Copyright © 2020 by Lucinda Jones
All rights reserved

Library of Congress Control Number: 2020908456
International Standard Guide Number: 978-0-9707826-1-8

Printed in the United States by Morris Publishing®
3212 East Highway 30
Kearney, NE 68847
1-800-650-7888

I want to express my gratitude to:

Elder Roy Haynes: for listening to my vision to write this book and for giving me his blessing.

Apostle O'Shay Smith: for prophesying five years ago that I would minister in the law.

Rachel Boyd: for interceding for me over the years and petitioning God on my behalf.

My Father and Siblings: for helping me to be the person I've become.

Issues In The Heart

Contents

A Personal Note vii
Preface ix

Part I – Introduction of Issues 1
1   Guard Your Heart 2

Part II – I.R.A.C. 7

2   The Issue 8
3   The Rule of Law 11
4   The Analysis 15
5   The Conclusion 23

Part III – Case Scenarios 25

6   Woman with the Issue of Blood 26
7   Miriam's and Aaron's Contempt 34
8   Accusers of the Adulterous Woman 38
9   Nebuchadnezzar's Fall 44
10 The Other Two Men on the Cross 50
11 Saul Envies David 54
12 Herod's Weakness 59
13 David's Hidden Sin 63
14 The Fishing Expedition 67
15 The Kids That Teased Elisha 71

Part IV – Writing the Analysis and Conclusion 75
16 Identifying Solutions 76

Part V - Worksheets 79

Issue 80
Rule of Law 82
Facts 84
Analysis 88
Conclusion 92

    Final Note 95

Issues In The Heart

A Personal Note

> *"One summer night, I awoke to voices and a light that filled the hallway that led to the bedroom that my sisters and I shared. Local police officers had entered our home, searching for a man that was wanted. I was only 9 and didn't know the law. But, I knew there was something wrong about the way the officers entered our home. At that moment, a fire was ignited in me. The spirit of advocacy was birthed in me."* - Lucinda Jones, Esq.

I am so glad God touched my heart that night.

Little did I know it was the beginning of a plan that he had established for my life, even before I was born. God was preparing me for ministry to advocate for others – to help people manage life's issues and attain wholeness from brokenness.

For how would I understand them unless I walked in their shoes?

For many years, I struggled to overcome hurt and pain from events that occurred in my life, beginning as a child. It left an open door for issues to develop. The issues controlled my emotions, my thoughts, and my desires. The consequences of them controlling me brought me to a state of emotional and spiritual brokenness. And, God came to my rescue.

I am a witness that anyone needing to get whole can get there. It wouldn't matter if you created your circumstances or not. God has already factored in the potential for error. I certainly have had my share of self-inflicted wounds. Yet, God overlooked my deficiencies, and He continued to work with me. He helped me to get control of my issues and attain wholeness. For that, I am humbly grateful.

BeBe and CeCe Winans sing a song: "*I.O.U. Me.*"

That song describes where I am in my life today. My hope is for people to be emotionally and spiritually whole. That's all that matters at the end of the day. For that reason, I have committed my works to Christ.

And, one other thought, what we say and what we do impacts how others feel at the end of the day. Let us ask God to help us do and say those things that edify.

Preface

*I*t was the 1960's, the era of the civil rights movement. Even at 9, I was bothered by the discrimination that African Americans endured at that time. God put a desire in my heart to address the injustice. I was too young to do anything that could have made an impact. But my passion nonetheless was strong. What was already a resounding yes to God's tug on my heart to be an advocate for others, I later resolved that I would go to law school and obtain a license, so that I could litigate injustice in the court.

And I did that.

For 24 years, I litigated civil rights matters in the federal courts, seeking redress on behalf of individuals that had experienced discrimination. My objective was always to help each of my clients achieve wholeness. In most cases, money awards were requested on behalf of the client to compensate him or her for damages they sustained. Additionally, money awards deterred the entity or individual from engaging in egregiousness and punitive actions that resulted in harm to the person suing. And, while these awards provide some relief to the individual, without more, they do not make the person whole.

Issues In The Heart

The truth be told, people want to experience emotional and spiritual wholeness in their lives today.

We have this saying: "If you don't have your physical health, you don't have anything."

There is truth in this statement!

It is also true that when an individual is not healthy emotionally and spiritually, it is challenging for them to navigate through life even with a physically fit body.

So, you want to hear another truth?

Peoples' emotions and spirits are broken by circumstances and events that occurred and are occurring in their lives. And these circumstances and events create issues in individuals' lives that make navigating life more challenging.

Have you been there? I have, and it is a tough place to be.

At 6, I was molested by two perpetrators, at different times. I also experienced verbal abuse during my childhood. The effect of these events caused me pain that I struggled with for years. As a result of the pain, a door was opened for issues to develop in my life: promiscuity, confusion, distrust. These issues controlled me for 30 years. Thirty years from the first abuse, God fully and completely delivered me. He brought me to a place of wholeness.

So, life issues, we all have them. And, if you haven't been

faced with one yet, be sure that you will. The Bible warns us to be on guard for them: "Keep thy heart with all diligence; for out of it are the issues of life." --Proverbs 4:23.

However, God never intended for your issues to control you. He wants you to master them.

He helped me master mine. How? By applying His Word and employing litigation strategy.

These concepts can help you master your issues, too.

Let me introduce you to *Issues In The Heart*."

"*Issues In The Heart*" will be your Development Guide (DG). It will help you manage issues that are problematic in your life. It includes Bible verses that reflect what God said about you in His law. And any problematic issue that you face must get in line with God's Word. Because God's Word is the law and his law is the truth. --Psalms 119:142.

As a participant, you will witness God's Word and litigation practices collaborate to bring into control the most used weapon the devil uses to frustrate man and keep him separated from God: issues. I teach you litigation strategy that I employ in my work as a civil rights attorney and that I teach as an instructor of paralegal studies. It includes case scenarios that demonstrate how God's Word and legal strategy are applied. It provides worksheets for you to analyze any issue(s) you are experiencing. We will discuss the analysis shortly.

This litigation strategy above is I.R.A.C. This acronym stands for:

Issue

Rule of Law

Analysis

Conclusion

Here's an overview of how I.R.A.C. works:

First, you will identify the issue. Succinctly state the item that is problematic to you.

Merriam-Webster defines an issue as:

1. A problem or concern;

2. A matter that is in dispute between two or more parties;

3. The point at which an unsettled question is ready for a decision.

This DG mainly addresses issues from an emotional and spiritual perspective. It does not dismiss the existence of physical problems. The same principle and strategy you are about to read are also useful for seeking and obtaining physical wholeness. An example is the *"Woman with the Issue of Blood."* We'll talk more about her in Part III.

Second, you will identify the Bible scripture that is responsive to your issue. It is the applicable (Law) that rules over the issue.

This scripture is the Rule of Law.

Third, you will analyze your case. The analysis is a two-fold process. It will require that you write down the facts that are relevant to your problem. It will not be a time to "cherry-pick." You must place all relevant facts "on the table." The second part will require that you examine them. Your inspection must be detailed. It requires honest self-inspection and sincere scrutiny. This thoroughness is necessary for you to obtain optimal results.

Don't sweat whether you'll be ready to analyze your case. The DG will help prepare you. It includes Bible stories that are analyzed using the I.R.A.C. process. See the Case Scenarios in Part II. You will have read them before you start to write your analysis.

Lastly, you will reach your conclusion. After you have "diligently" analyzed the facts of your case [emphasis added], you should have gained insight as to why the issue is problematic or troublesome to you. Prayerfully, you will successfully address it.

After you have finished reading *"Issues In The Heart,"* you'll know that you don't have to live with anything contrary to what God said about you.

Issues In The Heart

"For I know the thoughts that I think toward you, saith the LORD, thoughts of peace, and not of evil, to give you an expected end." --Jeremiah 29:11

You'll know that no issue is so big and so bad that it can dethrone God's law.

".... When the enemy shall come in like a flood, the Spirit of the LORD shall lift up a standard against him." --Isaiah 59:19

You'll know that for every issue that arises in your life, you have the power to master each of them.

"I can do all things through Christ which strengtheneth me." --Philippians 4:13

Now, let's get to work!

Part I: Introduction of Issues

1

Guard Your Heart

The heart is a vital organ.

Wouldn't you agree?

It pumps blood, delivers oxygen and nutrients to the tissues. It removes carbon dioxide and waste. Consuming healthy meals, exercising, and maintaining a manageable stress level assists the heart in maintaining its viability and strength. With a weak and unhealthy heart, man is vulnerable to disease and he could even die.

Man has a spiritual heart. It is the place where his desire (what he wants), his emotion (what he feels), and his intellect (what he thinks), begin. In other words, desire, emotion, and intellect are residents of the heart. Life issues want to enter the heart and influence these residents negatively.

By illustration let's give the heart a more formal name, Mr. Heart. He is the owner and overseer of his residence.

Now, let's say the issue of covetousness arises. Its intent is to influence Mr. Heart.

One definition of covetousness is having an inordinate desire for wealth or possessions - *Merriam-Webster*.

Covetousness goes to Mr. Heart's residence with the intent of influencing him to desire a mansion. He wants to live in one after he learns that someone else that he knows resides in one.

How successful covetousness is will depend on how well Mr. Heart's residence is protected. Does a superior spiritual security alarm defend it? Is Mr. Heart alert and recognizes that covetousness is on his premises? Does he panic?

Is God's law…"*Thou shall not covet*" --Exodus 20:17 ignited in him? Does he assert the authority of the law against covetousness? If he does, then he will have disarmed covetousness and expelled it from his residence (his heart). He has mastered it through God's command. Mr. Heart remains content living in the home that he now occupies.

Issues In The Heart

Let's say covetousness breaches Mr. Heart's desire. His defense strategy will determine the level of damage that occurred, if any. Mr. Heart starts to think about wanting to move into a mansion. But, then, he remembers the law on covetousness. He acknowledges the wrong of his thinking and drops that thought. He remains happy where he is. Mr. Heart is still in control.

What happens if Mr. Heart does not come into accord with the law concerning covetousness? His desire to have a mansion will control him. He will go broke trying to buy a more stately residence. He may even get sick working excessive overtime to pay for it. Now, he has multiplied his problems. He is certain to develop new issues.

It's best to master these issues immediately. And it starts with guarding your heart. *Keep thy heart with all diligence; for out of it are the issues of life."*-- Proverbs 4:23.

Merriam-Webster defines diligence as:
1. Steady;
2. Energetic effort;
3. Persevering application.

Do you get the idea?

It takes discipline and steadiness to keep the desire, emotion, and intellect in line with God's law. No one should be lazy or relaxed about it. No! You've got to be on guard…24/7. You've got to be diligent.

Diligence includes using your spiritual tools, such as reading God's Word, praying, fasting, and meditation. These are all good. But, please don't forget to use the weapon of common sense.

Let's illustrate.

Let's say an individual has a problem with gossip. He or she wants to get a handle on this issue. They should employ whatever spiritual weapon that is available to them. The one common sense weapon the individual can use is to tell the other person that he or she is not going to gossip anymore. An alternative is not to answer the telephone when the person calls. Sooner or later, they'll get the hint. But, it would be best that the individual directly communicated this. That way, the other side can think about the wrong in gossiping.

You are probably saying: "It's not that easy." And you are probably right. But, it takes this level of diligence and more to master your issues.

Issues In The Heart

The good news is that it's doable with God's help.

Part II:
I.R.A.C.

2

The Issue

At the center of every problem or dispute is an issue. It is the basis of every lawsuit that the Plaintiff files with the Court. It is called a Complaint. The Plaintiff is the individual that files the lawsuit. The Defendant is the individual sued.

In her written Complaint, the Plaintiff must set forth the issue. What was the Defendant's action that caused her to sue him? The Defendant's conduct must have violated a law or statute.

The Plaintiff's failure to state the issue could result in the dismissal of her claim. This would likely happen because the Defendant filed a motion asking the Court to dismiss the lawsuit. Or the Court could have dismissed the lawsuit sua sponte (on its own volition).

Now, can you imagine God not hearing your case on the ground that you didn't state your issue, or you didn't state it succinctly? It's unimaginable. You see, you don't have to have excellent communication skills to articulate your problem to God. God knows your heart. And He can discern your thoughts, even before you think them.

"Thou knowest my downsitting and mine uprising, thou understandest my thought afar off."

--Psalm 139:2.

Another thing, God would not dismiss your case because of some legal technicality. There is no such thing in the Kingdom of God. That's not God's nature. All He expects is that when you petition him to believe He will help you.

"If ye shall ask any thing in my name, I will do it."

--John 14:14

Yes! It's that simple!

Remember, any issue you have isn't big or bad enough that you can't master it with God's help.

Issues In The Heart

Please write out your issue in the Worksheet section on page 80, entitled "Issue." It is fresh in your mind right now, and it's genuinely flowing. You may have multiple issues. And that's okay. Write them down.

3

The Rule of Law

Laws are everywhere. They guide us and instruct us on how we should conduct ourselves in places, in transactions, and dealings. Each of us, including government and private actors, are accountable under the law.

The Plaintiff must state the "operative law" in her Complaint. In other words, she must cite the law that supports or answers the issue at hand. For example, if the Plaintiff alleges the Defendant assaulted her, she must invoke the applicable legislation concerning the assault.

This legislation is the Rule of Law.

When the Court assesses the Plaintiff's case to determine its merit, the Judge will look to the law that the Plaintiff cited. The Defendant will also state the law that he will rely on in defending the lawsuit against him. The Court could reject the rule that both parties cited. In the Plaintiff's case, it would likely be because the facts as presented by her did not persuade the Judge that the Defendant violated the law. And, visa versa, the Defendant's argument may not influence the Court that he did not violate the law.

The truth is man's Rule of Law is not perfect. And, judges are not flawless either. And, both being imperfect, sometimes the end results make the Rule of Law ineffective.

But God's law, on the other hand, is infallible. *His judgment is righteous. His law is truth.*

--Psalm 119:142.

And, because God's grace abounds, He is ready to forgive a man when he violates His law. Unlike human-made laws that are generally unforgiving and encourage punishment, God's law helps man live in line with His Word.

So, when you ascertain the biblical law that applies to your situation, don't be intimidated by it. Don't shy away from it. Approach this process with the expectation that God is going to help you master your issue. Also, be willing to make any adjustment the Lord may ask you to make.

After you have identified the law, the next step is analyzing your case. This step will bring you closer to understanding your issue and gaining insight on how to address it.

Please write out the Rule of Law in the Worksheet section on page 82, entitled "Rule of Law."

Remember, you are looking for the law that applies to your issue. Also, if you have multiple problems, you should have matching rules.

This exercise may require research on your part. Biblegateway.com is a good source. To find the applicable law, identify keywords that are associated with your issue. For example, if depression is an issue, type the term "depression" in the Biblegateway.com search engine. Strong Concordance is another source.

No worries, only you will see the results.

4

The Analysis

A detailed examination of the facts by the Plaintiff is critical in the I.R.A.C. analysis. Why? They will aid the Court in determining whether the law supports her claims. Thus, Plaintiff should make a painstaking effort to ensure she has obtained and provided all the relevant and material facts to the Court. And, it starts with discovery.

Discovery is the heart of the lawsuit. It is the best shot for the Plaintiff to make her case and survive any challenge by the Defendant. It is a process whereby the attorney requests that their opponent (or the other side) answers questions and produce documents. Each party will be required to provide the answers and materials to the opposing counsel. Once the parties have collected the information, they can file their dispositive Motion.

This Motion, entitled Motion for Summary Judgment, is usually filed by the Defendant. The

Defendant is asking the Court to rule in his favor on the ground Plaintiff's Complaint fails to state a genuine issue of material fact.

A material fact is defined as follows:

> The word "material" means that the subject matter of the statement [or concealment] related to a fact or circumstance which would be important to the decision to be made as distinguished from an insignificant, trivial or unimportant detail: *The Lectric Law Library, LECTLAW.COM.*

In his Motion, the Defendant will present his facts. He must support each point with the material in the record. The Plaintiff will respond. She will either admit each of the Defendant's statements or deny them, also pointing to the evidence. Additionally, she will present her separate facts.

Ideally, she will pack her response with statements of material facts. Her goal is to state as many material facts as possible to bolster her claim and refute the

Defendant's facts. To survive the Defendant's Motion for Summary Judgment, Plaintiff only needs to present one genuine issue of material fact.

Do you see the significance of presenting material facts in this process?

Now that the Court has the Defendant's Motion and the Plaintiff's response, it can now start analyzing the case. By this time, the Court has a grasp of the issue and the rule of law. The Judge will meticulously examine the facts, looking for material facts that are relevant to the question and the law.

The Court will weigh the facts with the law, whether the law supports the Plaintiff's claim. Did the facts persuade the Court to believe that the Defendant did what the Plaintiff alleged? Were the facts the Defendant presented sufficient to satisfy the Court otherwise?

In a nutshell, the Court's adjudication hinges on the presence or the absence of material facts.

You will be conducting a self-analysis, as described above.

The touchstone of the analysis is being honest with your-self and being forthcoming about the facts.

You must adhere to this scrutiny for the review to be beneficial to you.

You must be willing to place all of the facts on the table, and you must examine them objectively. It may feel like digging an old sore open. It could hurt and probably will. But, it is necessary to get to the root of your issue so that you can understand why it is problematic. You'll be able to identify viable solutions to help you master it.

Remember, the analysis is a two-step process. You will write out your facts and write the examination.

Now, you can expect it to be challenging. One, because the facts you will document will be about you. Again, you are encouraged to be forthcoming. No one sees this but you unless you share it with someone else. You may even consider having someone that you know and someone that identifies with you to write out your facts. Having someone else write it would enhance objectivity. But make sure it's someone that you "love and trust" to the utmost, someone who has been "tried and tested."

Secondly, it will be equally challenging to analyze you. You must be willing to be critical of yourself. You must be willing to accept any found deficiencies. Or, you could have someone else to write it, as suggested above. Whoever writes the analysis, they should thoroughly vet the facts. Hopefully, the result of your examination is that your story is per God's Rule of Law.

Ask yourself questions after you've conducted your analysis, such as: How did my story measure? Is it in accordance with the law? Are there any adjustments I can make to bring my life in line with the law?

By illustration, let's say your story involves the issue of worry. The corresponding Rule of Law is: *"Trust in the LORD with all thine heart; and lean not unto thine own understanding."* --Proverb 3:5.

What does your story reveal about your state of mind? Does it let you know whether you trust Jesus? Do you focus on Jesus when circumstances that would make you worry arise? Or do you worry about what could happen? What adjustments can you make that will help you to trust God and believe what He said?

If you have vetted your facts well, you should get some revelation and some answers.

One thing you can be sure of, when you analyze your issue relying on God's laws, you can only win. But, you must present your entire case to Him. He knows your circumstances, anyways. He wants you to acknowledge them.

The Analysis consists of two parts – the facts and the actual writing of your examination.

Please write out your facts in the Worksheet section on page 84, entitled "Facts." Write them down while they are fresh in your mind and flowing in your head. You can always return and add facts that you later recollect.

At this juncture, don't be concerned whether the facts you write down are relevant or material. Write down every event that comes to mind. When you write your examination, then you will include only material facts.

PLEASE DO NOT WRITE THE ANALYSIS YET. Read the Conclusion on page 23. After you have finished the Conclusion, begin reading the Case Scenarios in Part III.

After you have read the cases, you will write the Analysis and the Conclusion.

5

The Conclusion

Remember, you will write your Conclusion after you have completed your Analysis.

By the time you have done so you will have gotten to the root of your issue. You will understand why it's been problematic for you. Most importantly, you will be able to identify viable solutions to help you master it.

Now, start reading the Case Scenarios beginning in Part III, Page 25.

.

Issues In The Heart

Part III:
Case Scenarios

6

Woman with the Issue of Blood

Can you imagine bleeding for twelve years? No help. No cure.

Then Jesus comes.

Facts.

This woman had been sick for a long time. She had an issue of blood for 12 years. During this period, she received medical treatment from many physicians. They tested and examined her. But, they could not cure her. She was required to pay for these services. She spent all that she had on getting better. But, her health did not improve. Instead, she got worse.

She had heard of Jesus. He was coming through her town. On His way there, He cast evil spirits out of a man. He permitted them to enter swine that fed nearby. They were 2000 in number. After Jesus left that miracle He journeyed by ship toward the woman's town.

Many people met Jesus as He exited the ship. As Jesus walked by, the woman pressed into the crowd from behind. For she said if she could touch His clothes, she would be made whole. Immediately after her touching Jesus, her blood dried up. She felt healed in her body.

And Jesus became aware that someone had touched Him because virtue had gone out of Him. Jesus asked who touched His clothes. The woman trembled and fell before Jesus. He turned to her and said:

Issues In The Heart

> *"Daughter, thy faith hath made thee whole; go in peace, and be whole of thy plague."*
> --Mark 5:1-34

Issue 1: Why was the woman's healing delayed?

Rule of Law: "Have faith in God."
--Mark 11:22.

Analysis: Why did it take so long for the woman to get healed? Did she know about faith? Perhaps she did, but the heaviness of her burdens overwhelmed her and discouraged her from pursuing faith any further. Or maybe she did have faith, but it had not developed to the level where she could receive her healing. Whatever her level of confidence was, one day, she heard about Jesus and His healing powers. She learned He was coming to her town. It increased her hope.

Can you imagine the woman's reaction when she heard Jesus was close to her neighborhood? Imagine her just having listened to the news about the devils Jesus had just cast out of the man. To understand that by Jesus' authority, they entered into two-thousand swine must have been encouraging.

Hearing these events must have ignited the woman's faith.

After Jesus exited the ship bringing Him from where the miracle took place, crowds began to gather and throng Him. The woman probably stood afar off so not to be noticed. She knew Jesus was a man that people reverenced. She likely rehearsed in her heart how she would approach Him. She prepared in her mind how Jesus would respond.

Her eyes desperately veered through the people that surrounded Jesus. She could see Jesus walking through the crowd – her eyes locked onto the hem of His garment. She was not timid but was confident and moved with urgency.

The woman's hope that had developed into muster seed faith by then had become faith on spiritual steroids.

She reasoned to herself if she could touch His clothes she would be made whole. She felt it would probably be the only time in a long time, if ever again, that she'd get this opportunity. No, she was not going to let this opportunity escape her. In desperation, she moved more assertively towards Jesus.

She ignored the whispers and taunts, probably people calling her "unclean," "unclean." Her growing faith consoled her and gave her the strength and the audacity to continue moving forward. She kept pressing into the crowd from behind, and she finally touched the hem of Jesus' garment. Immediately her fountain of blood dried up. And, she knew Jesus had healed her.

Jesus asked: "Who touched my clothes?" He recognized that of all the hands that touched Him, this one was different. It was a commanding touch, so commanding that it tapped into His power and withdrew from it. He knew a spiritual withdrawal had occurred because virtue left Him.

Moreover, Jesus was astonished by the person's bodacious act of faith. He looked around to find this person. He laid His eyes on the woman. In reverent fear, she fell before Jesus. He acknowledged that her faith had made her whole and commanded that she go in peace and be made whole of her issue of blood.

Conclusion: The woman was healed of her issue of blood because she had faith. When she touched Jesus' garment, she consummated her faith. Her faith made her whole. All you need is muster seed faith to be made whole.

Jesus cured the woman's issue of blood. What about her emotional wholeness? It was a secondary problem.

Issue: Was the woman emotionally broken? If so, did she receive emotional healing after she touched the hem of Jesus' garment?

Rule of Law: "He healeth the broken heart, and bindeth up their wounds." --Psalm 147:3.

Analysis: The facts suggest the woman was emotionally broken. It started with her issue of blood.

According to Moses' law, a woman who was on her menstrual cycle was unclean, and she was set apart from the public. --Leviticus 15:19-25. Her separation was for seven days. If it continued beyond seven days, she was deemed unclean for the entire period her issue flowed. And anyone that touched her was considered unclean.

Undoubtedly, the woman endured loneliness for twelve years. Imagine her set apart from her family and friends and not being able to socialize with them, much less touch them. How on special celebrations and holidays that she traditionally enjoyed with her loved ones, she sat alone, only able to view the events from her window? Or she watched from a place reserved for the unclean.

Now, add the feeling of shame and hurt from people that shunned her. Likely, the by-passers shrugged their noses up at her, and the town's bully children threw rocks at her calling her "unclean," "unclean."

The woman sought medical treatment from multiple physicians. Given the educational and social status of women, then, these gynecologists were likely male. Now, that probably caused her stress, on another level. How did they treat her? Did they view her as a second class citizen? Did her status as an unclean woman cause them to look at her negatively? Imagine the shame and humiliation she must have felt being examined by these male gynecologists.

But, what is pivotal to whether the woman had become emotionally and spiritually broken is how she fell at Jesus' feet and told Him her story. It must have been a great relief for her, first, to touch someone and have them not mind being touched by her. Secondly, she was able to vent. She told Jesus all twelve years of pain, loneliness, and humiliation.

There is no doubt that the woman's experience left her emotionally broken. But, Jesus did not leave her in that state. He healed her heart and bound up her emotional wounds, as well as her plague.

Conclusion: When Jesus heals an individual, He makes them whole. He makes them complete.

7

Miriam's and Aaron's Contempt

Moses, Miriam, and Aaron were siblings. Following Moses' lead, they ministered well together. Then, Moses married the Ethiopian woman.

Facts:

Moses married an Ethiopian. Miriam and Aaron spoke against Moses because of the Ethiopian woman whom he had married.

Then, they questioned whether the LORD had spoken only by Moses. They touted that the Lord had also spoken by them.

The LORD heard what they said, and He became angry. As a result, the Lord struck Miriam with leprosy. She grew white as snow. Moses asked the Lord to remove the disease from Miriam, but He would not. Instead, He required that she be leprous for seven days. As a result, she was set apart from the camp and her people.
--Numbers 12:1-16

Issue: Did Miriam and Aaron have Respect of Persons.

Rule of Law: "For there is no respect of persons with God." --Romans 2:11

Analysis: What was up with Miriam and Aaron? By all accounts, they were Moses' right and left hand. Aaron was Moses' mouthpiece. He accompanied Moses to Egypt to obtain the release of the Israelites from the bondage of the Pharaoh. Miriam, the prophetess, celebrated her brother when he, by the power of God, caused the red sea to open up so that the Israelites could walk to the other side. They witnessed God accomplish great things through Moses. And, they didn't question His authority.

And, then Miriam and Aaron spoke against Moses' wife because she was an Ethiopian. They questioned whether the Lord spoke only through Moses. They touted that God spoke through them, too.

Why did they, now, have this contempt for Moses?

Had they become bitter because Moses married this Ethiopian woman? Was it because her origin and ethnicity were different than Moses' background? Was it because she had a darker complexion? Did they have a disdain for her culture?

Were they suggesting that God did not authorize Moses to marry the woman because she was Ethiopian?

Whatever their reason, they disrespected Moses and his wife. Their actions were also rebellion against God. And for that, God became angry. He struck Miriam with leprosy, and she became white as snow. God expressed fiery disdain with Moses concerning Miriam's disrespect. Even Moses, who had persuaded

God in time past not to slaughter the Israelites because of their disobedience, he could not get God to reverse His decision concerning Miriam. And, God shut her out of the camp for seven days, the term of her leprosy.

Was God teaching a lesson of respect? Miriam of all people...she was a prophetess. People in the camp looked up to her. By striking her with leprosy, was God teaching the people that Church status did not give a license to sin?

Was He denouncing discrimination and racism based on skin color and ethnicity? Did He want Miriam to experience the feeling of differential treatment? So she would learn how it felt to be an outcast?

Was God showing the people His sovereignty that He does whatever pleases Him, and He uses who He wants for his pleasure?

Conclusion. Who is a man to question what God has ordained? It is dangerous. It appears Miriam got the lesson. After she had completed her seven days of leprosy, the camp resumed its journey, and she traveled with them.

8

Accusers of the Adulterous Woman

The woman got caught in the act of adultery. Jesus challenged her accusers, and He ended up pardoning her sin.

Facts:

Early in the morning, Jesus was in the temple teaching. As He taught, the scribes and Pharisees brought a woman before Him who had just engaged in adultery. They told Jesus the woman was *"taken in adultery, in the very act."* Tempting Jesus, they asked Him if she should be put to death according to Moses' law. They hoped to accuse Him.

Jesus stooped down and

with His finger started writing on the ground, as though He did not hear them. They continued to ask Jesus if the woman deserved death.

Finally, Jesus got up and He said to them: *"He that is without sin among you, let him first cast a stone at her."* Then, he stooped down and continued writing on the ground again.

When Jesus stood, everyone was gone but the woman. No man had condemned her. And neither did Jesus. He told her to *"go, and sin no more."*
--John 8:1-11.

Issue: Did the scribes and Pharisees have the right to Judge the woman?

Rule of Law: "Judge not, that ye be not judged." --Matthew 7:1

Analysis: It is easy to judge others, mainly when the accused is guilty of the act. But, it's not cool when the accuser is guilty of doing the same thing.

Is that what happened here?

There was, indeed, something amiss about how the scribes and Pharisees accused the woman. First, they brought her to Jesus while He was conducting a bible study. Right there, in the middle of the sanctuary floor, they cast down the woman. Could this not have waited until Jesus finished teaching?

Secondly, it doesn't appear the scribes and Pharisees were righteously indignant that the woman had violated the law. No. They planned to discredit Jesus, and embarrass Him. It was no secret that they did not like Jesus. They loathed Him; He was smart, bold, and people revered Him. He was probably handsome, too; He looked better than them on any "bad hair day." But He was most hated because He was a truth-teller.

The scribes and Pharisees wanted to accuse Jesus. If Jesus had not agreed with them that the woman deserved death, they would have accused Him of being a lawbreaker. Moses' law required death. --Leviticus 20:10. If Jesus had agreed with them, they likely would have accused Him of being noncompliant with His practices. He had forgiven others' sin in time past. These men wanted to be "validated" as "spiritual authorities." And this was their opportunity to make it happen.

But it appears Jesus had concerns that if the people executed the woman, her death would have resulted in grave injustice to the fundamentals of fairness and equity.

Why would fairness and equity have been a concern to Jesus?

Were the scribes and Pharisees complicit? How is it that they came to learn that the woman was committing adultery? Were they physically there? Did they, themselves, actually catch her in the act? Or did something more sinister happen? Was Jesus considering these things as He contemplated His response?

The scribes and Pharisees were adamant that Jesus answers the fate of the woman. Pretending like He didn't hear them, Jesus stooped to the ground and started writing. They even harassed Jesus as He wrote on the ground.

What did Jesus write? We don't know. But could He have written, probably, what He was thinking:

God is not mocked. **Hypocrites!** **Get the beam out of your eye.**

After Jesus finished writing He got up, and He challenged anyone who was without sin to cast a stone at the woman. The scribes and Pharisees were not going to take no for an answer.

Then, Jesus lowered Himself to the ground and wrote some more.

Why did He write again? Was He giving the scribes and Pharisees time to consider the matter and walk away with some integrity intact?

Maybe He was.

And what did He write?

Whatever He wrote, it shut the whole matter down. When He got up, this time, all of the woman's accusers were gone. He instructed the woman to go and not to sin again.

Conclusion: It's not that the scribes and Pharisees did not have grounds to bring the accusation against the woman. She violated the law. But they judged her out of malice because they hated Jesus. And, they were not in a position to judge the woman or anyone else because their lives were not sin-free.

9

Nebuchadnezzar's Fall

Nebuchadnezzar, the King of Babylon, God made him great. He besieged Jerusalem, and God gave the King of Judah into his hands. Then, Nebuchadnezzar credited himself for his success.

Facts:

> In the second year that Nebuchadnezzar reigned, he dreamed about a high image that troubled his spirit. None of his magicians, astrologers, or sorcerers could interpret it. Daniel, Shadrach, Meshach, and Abednego, prayed that God would give Daniel the vision. God did.
>
> Daniel told the King that he was the image that he saw in the dream. And

that God had given him a Kingdom, power, and strength, and glory. Nebuchadnezzar made an image of gold, and he ordered the nations to worship the image. Those who did not worship would be cast into a fiery furnace.

Nebuchadnezzar had a second dream, this time of a strong-tall tree. The tree lost its strength and vitality. Daniel told Nebuchadnezzar that he would fall and be driven from his Kingdom to dwell with animals and eat grass as oxen until he knew that God ruled. Daniel urged the King to repent and turn to God.

Twelve months later, Nebuchadnezzar boasted how he had built his Kingdom by the might of his power, and for the honor of his majesty. And as he spoke, a voice from heaven said: "Oh king Nebuchadnezzar, to thee it is spoken; The

Kingdom is departed from thee." As a result, Nebuchadnezzar was driven from his Kingdom and lived with the beast, according to Daniel's interpretation.

After Nebuchadnezzar understood that God reigned, he blessed and praised him. God restored Nebuchadnezzar to his Kingdom and added excellent majesty to him.
--Daniel 1, 2, 3, 4.

Issue: Did Nebuchadnezzar walk in pride?

Rule of Law: "Pride goeth before destruction, and a haughty spirit before a fall." --Proverbs 16:18

Analysis: Nebuchadnezzar found favor in God. God made him a powerful King, and he, no doubt, had everything that he wanted. He besieged Jerusalem, and God delivered the king of Judah into his hand. Nebuchadnezzar had access to Jerusalem's archives, treasures, and peoples. For example, he had Daniel, Shadrach, Meshach, and Abednego brought from the

Jerusalem camp into his palace. They were significant assets to his Kingdom.

Nebuchadnezzar even took pleasures in calling on other gods through magic, astrology, and sorcery, without any immediate repercussion from God. He had done it so long he probably thought it was alright to continue. Besides, God was blessing him anyway. At least, that's perhaps was how he felt.

And, God gave Nebuchadnezzar a dream about himself. Daniel told him how his Kingdom would be mighty and would flourish. No doubt, this prophecy further bolstered the legitimacy and efficacy of Nebuchadnezzar's Kingdom. The message did come from God. But, did it give him the "big head?" Did he, now, believe that he was invincible? Perhaps, even immortal?

Is that why Nebuchadnezzar built an image of gold and ordered the nations to worship it? Was he that much into himself and self-confident to order the death of people by fire because they did not worship him? Daniel, Chapter 3 reveals that Shadrach, Meshach, and Abednego were thrown into the furnace because they refused to worship the image. Nebuchadnezzar had to have known that they refused

Issues In The Heart

to bow down because they worshipped their God only. Perhaps, that's why he had the heat turned up seven times.

What did God feel about this? Evidence suggests God still favored Nebuchadnezzar. For one thing, God revealed Jesus to Nebuchadnezzar when he looked into the furnace. He saw a fourth image walking with Shadrach, Meshach, and Abednego, whom he said "is like the Son of God." The only way Nebuchadnezzar could have known that is if God revealed it to him. How many people had had that experience, much less a worldly King?

God gave Nebuchadnezzar another dream. Daniel, again, gave the interpretation. This time, it foretold of Nebuchadnezzar's fall because of his pride. Daniel urged him to repent of his sins and to be kind to the oppressed. Yet, the King doubled down. Twelve months later he boasted about how he made Babylon great. Consequently, God ousted him from his Kingdom and deduced him to an animal grazing in the grass.

What a terrible fall from glory. What did Nebuchadnezzar think while he was in that state? He probably was shocked that this would happen to him...to go from eating steak on a silver platter to eating worms in the earth. From sleeping on silk sheets to being covered with the grass dew...what a terrible fall from grace. And why did he remain in that state for seven years?

Could he have come out sooner? Well, he came out when he came to himself. He realized that God is God and that there is none other than Him. That God places man wherever He chooses, for His pleasure, and He brings him down.

Yes! Nebuchadnezzar finally got it.

Conclusion: Pride can blind a person to the source of their success. God restored Nebuchadnezzar to greatness, and even more because he debased himself and honored God as the only King.

10

The Other Two Men on The Cross

At Calvary were three crosses. One was for Jesus and two other men who had been adjudged criminals. One asked for forgiveness – the other one did not.

Facts:

A company of people and women wailed and lamented Jesus as He made His way to Calvary. He was about to endure the finality of His execution by being nailed to the cross.

Jesus, knowing His fate, asked His Father to forgive His crucifiers and those that scorned and mocked Him. He asked this because He knew they didn't understand what they were doing. The people and the rulers derided Jesus, saying He saved others but could not save Himself. The soldiers also mocked Him.

The unrepentant man that hung next to Jesus challenged Him, saying: "If thou be Christ, save thyself and us." The penitent man rebuked him and acknowledged that they were worthy of their punishment and that Jesus had done nothing wrong.

The penitent man asked Jesus to remember him when Jesus would be in His kingdom. Jesus told the man that He would remember him. After that the sun darkened, and the earth was dark for three hours. Also, the temple separated. Then, Jesus died.
--Luke 23:27-46

Issue: Did the unrepentant man have a problem asking for forgiveness?

Rule of Law: "Ask, and it shall be given you; seek, and ye shall find; knock, and it shall be opened unto you." --Matthew 7:7

Analysis: Two men are guilty of committing the same crime. As they hung on their cross on each side of Jesus, they witnessed the same events. One asked for forgiveness, and the other one did not.

Interestingly, the unrepentant man did not start railing against Jesus until after the crowd had ridiculed and mocked Him for a while. He joined the group after the rulers taunted Jesus. Was he a men pleaser hoping because he joined them in deriding Jesus they would let him down from the cross?

Or, was his heart hardened? How could it be? Didn't the wailing and lamenting of those that loved Jesus convince him that Christ was a man of great worth? Plus, he had just witnessed Jesus ask His Father to forgive His enemies. Jesus had just forgiven the penitent man by a simple request. He saw the earth become dark for three hours. Indeed, he could hear the cry from afar: "The temple is rent, the temple is rent"?

Certainly, he was reassessing the events and rethinking his position? And, what was he thinking during those three hours when the earth was dark? Was he scared? He likely wanted to ask Jesus to forgive him. But, how could he after how he treated Jesus earlier? It would make him look foolish before the people.

Did he have pride? If so, did it stop him from asking Jesus to forgive him?

Or, maybe he didn't believe in that Jesus stuff.

Whatever the man's stance, the time had run out for him to ask Jesus for forgiveness because Jesus predeceased him.

In contrast, the penitent man acknowledged his need for forgiveness. And, he asked Jesus to receive him into His Kingdom. Anything that he had done in his past that would have disqualified him from entering Jesus' Kingdom was forgiven immediately upon him asking.

Yes. It's just that simple.

Conclusion: There is no reason why anyone should not ask Jesus to forgive them. He is willing and ready to forgive. **Just ask Him!**

11

Saul Envies David

King Saul was obsessed with destroying David, starting from the time he killed Goliath.

Facts:

King Saul and the Israelites were at war with the Philistines. David was the youngest of eight brothers. His three oldest brothers were in Saul's army.

One day, David took food to the camp where his eldest brothers and the other soldiers were fighting. As David talked to the men, Goliath challenged them to choose a man to come down and fight with him. He was the Philistines' champion. King Saul and his army were afraid to fight the Philistines because of the size of Goliath. He was around 9 feet and 9 inches tall.

David volunteered to fight Goliath. David was youthful and red, and Goliath disdained him. David killed Goliath and cut off his head. Then, Israel and Judah pursued the Philistines and defeated them.

After David returned from killing Goliath, he stood before King Saul holding Goliath's head in his hand. Saul set David over the men of war. All of the people accepted David, and he behaved himself wisely.

As David came from defeating the Philistines, the women answered one another as they played, and said, Saul has killed his thousands and David his ten thousands. Saul was wroth and the saying displeased him. And, Saul eyed David from

Issues In The Heart

that day forward.
--I Samuel 17 and 18

Issue: Was Saul jealous of David?

Rule of Law: "Let us not be desirous of vain glory, provoking one another, envying one another."
--Galatians 5:26

Analysis: Evidence suggests Saul was jealous of David and envied him.

Initially, Saul was so impressed with David that he took him into his home and would not let him go back to his father's house. By all accounts, David reverenced Saul. He was respectful to him, and he obeyed him.

What made Saul so mad about David?

What would make a grown man, a beloved King, suddenly hate a young boy that he just loved a minute ago?

Was it because David volunteered to fight the champion Goliath when Saul and his army were afraid to challenge the Philistines? This likely embarrassed Saul. And, David's rejection of the armor Saul tried to fit him with likely further embarrassed Saul. Then, David took Goliath down with a pebble. That's enough to mess with any King's manhood. David, having a sincere and gentle spirit, probably realized this. So, he was careful not to appear arrogant after he beheaded Goliath. He didn't walk around toting Goliath's head, saying: "Hey, I just beheaded Goliath, the most wanted man in Jerusalem. I am the man." No. He took Goliath's head and humbly stood before King Saul.

Then, the nail of jealousy and envy sealed Saul's hatred for David.

The women came out to meet Saul and David to celebrate their success in defeating the Philistines. While playing musical instruments, they said Saul had killed his thousands and David his ten thousands. From that moment, Saul envied David.

Did the fact that David had killed Goliath and thousands more than Saul impact Saul's attitude? Had the women ever come out to praise Saul before? Did Saul foresee David reigning as King one day? Did all these things reduce him to jealousy?

Unfortunately, Saul pursued David's death for most of their relationship. He stopped pursuing David after David fled to Philistine territory, the city of Gath.

--1 Samuel 27:4.

Conclusion: Jealousy and envy are issues that can be deadly to an individual's well-being; they are akin to hate. They have no reasoning. But, the good news is that anyone can master this issue with God's help.

12

Herod's Weakness

King Herod and Herodias had lustful desires. John the Baptist lost his life because of their lust.

Facts:

Herod was Ruler of Galilee. He married his brother's wife, Herodias. John the Baptist told the King that it was not lawful for him to have his brother's wife. Herodias hated John the Baptist and would have killed him, but she could not. But, the King feared him knowing he was a just and holy man. He also gladly listened to John when he preached.

The King celebrated his birthday and made a supper for his guests. His guests were people of high estate. Herodias' daughter danced before the King, and it pleased him. He then promised the daughter he would give her anything she asked, even half of his Kingdom. The daughter went to her mother and asked her what she should ask. Herodias said the head of John the Baptist. With haste, the daughter went to the King and asked for the head of John.

King Herod was sorry for the oath he made. He immediately had an executioner behead John. The executioner put it in a charger and gave it to the daughter. The daughter, then, gave it to Herodias.
--Mark 6:17-28.

Issue: Were Herod and Herodias ruled by Lust?

Rule of Law: "This I say then, Walk in the Spirit, and ye shall not fulfill the lust of the flesh." Galatians --5:16.

Analysis: It appears King Herod was reeled in by lust. What type of man offers half of his kingdom to a young girl because she pleased him with her dance? Likely, he consumed alcoholic beverages during the festivities. No doubt, it enhanced his lustful appetite? And, this was not King Herod's first engagement with seduction. He married his brother's wife, Herodias. And, whether he lured her or she lured him, it amounted to a temptation that resulted in their union.

Deep down, did Herod know he was wrong by having his brother's wife? Was John's preaching reaching him down on the inside? He liked John. He even loved listening to John's sermons, despite John's criticism of him for having Herodias. But, Herod was in a difficult place. Even if he wanted to stop his lustful ways and live a Christian life, he was in an atmosphere that did not promote Christianity and wholesome living...starting with Herodias.

Herodias appeared to have a lustful appetite, herself. First, she left her husband for another man. Consider that she likely married Herod because it gave her wealth, status, and riches. Then she had her daughter to dance in front of Herod because she knew it would appeal to his sexuality. And, appealing to his sexuality, she knew the king would extend her daughter a wish for anything she wanted.

Did Herodias use sexuality to get revenge on John the Baptist?

***Conclusion*:** Unfortunately, King Herod and Herodias did not walk in the Spirit. Consequently, the desires of their flesh ruled their lives.

It takes walking in the Spirit to control this issue.

13

David's Hidden Sin

King David, a man after God's own heart, had an innocent man killed. And, he hid it until Nathan exposed it.

Facts:

God sent Nathan the prophet to talk to David. His conversation with David started with a parable:

Nathan:
There were two men in a city. One was rich, and the other one was poor. The rich man had many flocks, and the poor man had just a ewe lamb that he raised with his children. It was as a daughter to him. A traveler came to visit the rich man. He killed and cooked the poor man's

lamb and served it to the traveler. He spared his flock.

David became angry. He said to Nathan that the man who did this should surely die. And, that he shall restore the lamb fourfold because he did not have pity.

Nathan said to David, "Thou art the man." Nathan spoke of David's servant, Uriah, who fought in David's army. While Uriah was at war, David slept with Bathsheba, Uriah's wife. He impregnated her. After David learned of the pregnancy, he ordered the death of Uriah, to occur as he fought on the frontline. After his death, David married Bathsheba.

After Nathan finished his sayings, David confessed his wrong. Nathan told him the LORD had put away his sin, and he

14

The Fishing Expedition

The disciples grew weary because they had not made a day's catch. Then Jesus joined the crew.

Facts:

Jesus stood by the lake of Gennesaret. He saw two ships at the lake. The fishermen that owned them were washing their nets. Jesus sat in one of the vessels owned by Simon. He asked Simon to move the ship a little from the land so he could teach the people. After He finished teaching, He asked Simon to move his boat into the deep and let down his net.

Simon answered Jesus and said: "We have toiled all the night and

have taken nothing: nevertheless at thy word I will let down the net." Then, they caught a multitude of fish in their net that it broke. When Simon and his two partners brought their ship to land, they forsook everything and followed Jesus.
--Luke 5:1-11

Issue: Did Simon have anxiety?

Rule of Law: "Be careful for nothing; but in everything by prayer and supplication with thanksgiving, let your requests be made known unto God." --Philippians 4:6

Analysis: Jesus came to the lake of Gennesaret to witness to people and teach them the gospel. He stood by the lake, and He noticed two empty ships and their fisherman washing their net. That told Jesus that they had not caught any fish.

And, Jesus was aware that they needed a supply of fish to fill the marketplace from which they sold them. He knew He had to help them.

At the same time, Jesus devised a plan to help them and witness.

To make the connection with Simon, Jesus asked him if He could teach from his ship. Simon obliged Him. Simon was probably more concerned that he and his two partners did not catch fish. And, he was likely worried that they would not be able to make a living on tomorrow. Jesus knowing their anxiety probably touched on the subject matters of worrying and trusting God when he taught them. So, by the time Jesus finished teaching, their worries lessened.

After Jesus finished teaching, He asked Simon to move his ship into the deep and drop their net into the waters. Simon responded that they had been out all night and had not caught any fish, "nevertheless, at thy word I will let down the net." From Simon's response, any anxiety that he was experiencing dissipated. As a result of his obedience to Jesus' direction, he and his men caught more fish than their net could hold.

Simon and his two partners were so impressed with Jesus that when they brought their boat to land, they left everything and followed Him.

Conclusion: Anxiety and worry are not beneficial. Neither of these changes one's circumstances. Simon and his partners soon learned that. Through prayer and supplication, let Jesus know what you need. He'll answer you.

15

The Kids That Teased Elisha

Some kids are bullies and like to mess with people, especially older adults. But they messed with the wrong person that day.

Facts:

That day, Elijah had an appointment to relocate to heaven. God had it scheduled to take him to heaven by a whirlwind. As he and his servant Elisha walked along the way, Elijah asked him (Elisha) what he shall do for him before he went away. Elisha asked for a double portion of his spirit. Elijah granted the request, as long as Elisha could see him as he's taken away into heaven. As they walked, the whirlwind took Elijah

Issues In The Heart

up. Elisha picked up Elijah's mantle. On his way towards Bethel, he performed two miracles. He parted the waters to get to the other side and healed the city's water.

After these miracles, Elisha went his way. While traveling, little children came out of the city and mocked him, calling him bald head. Elisha looked back at them and cursed them in the name of the Lord. Two she-bears came out of the woods and killed 42 children of them.
--2 Kings 2

Issue: Did the children's disobedient dishonor their parents? Did their conduct result in their demise?

Rule of Law: "Children, obey your parents in the Lord. Honour thy father and mother; which is the first commandment with promise; That it may be well with thee, and thou mayest live long on the earth." -- Ephesians 6:1-3.

Analysis: Have you ever dealt with a bully child? Bully kids are well- rehearsed. They've been bullying for a long time. Their parents warn them about their behavior over and over again. But, they don't listen. They think they are invincible. Peer pressure and the insatiable desire to get a laugh at the expense of someone else are what drive them. The kids in this story are no different.

After Elisha healed the city's water, he began walking up the road. Dozens of kids came out of the city, and without any provocation by Elisha, they started harassing him. Likely, they surrounded him in a hasty manner that not only startled him but angered him. They called him bald head, bald head, and in essence, told him to get out of town. In his anger, Elisha turned around and cursed them in the name of the Lord. As a result, two she-bears heard Elisha's command, and came out of the woods and killed 42 children.

It appears there were other kids whose lives the bears spared. They were the fortunate ones. Maybe they were ones that didn't verbally attack Elisha, and they just went with the crowd and watched.

All these kids likely gave their parents or guardians a difficult time. They probably had rap sheets that revealed their previous trouble with the law. They had stolen, robbed, smoked weed, committed battery, and assault. Because they were juveniles, the system could only hold them temporarily and not long enough to rehabilitate them.

Not only did they have a duty to obey their parents or guardian, but they owed a duty to society to behave. And they didn't. Consequently, their lives were cut short way before its time.

Conclusion: Teens and adolescents, particularly those living with their parents, must follow the rules and instructions. And when they are no longer living under their parents' roof, they have an ongoing duty to obey society's rules and laws. And, when they fail to, life will be difficult for them. In other cases, their lives are susceptible to come to an early end.

So, hey kids, it's a smart thing to comply with all laws, especially God's.

Part IV: Writing the Analysis and Conclusion

16

Identifying Solutions

When identifying solutions, the first thing that probably comes to your mind is prayer, reading the Bible, and attending Church regularly. These are good, and they are necessary. Additionally, there are common-sense practices that you can incorporate into your solutions.

For example, an analyzed case might reveal to one that he or she can resolve the problem with professional and quality counseling. It may be the individual who needs to talk to someone and tell them about their troubles like the Woman with the Issue of Blood told Jesus.

Another individual might discover that he or she may need to purge toxic persons from their relationships.

Yet, another analysis might show that the individual needs to shut off the cable, at least until they can get the issue under control?

And, another analysis might reveal that the individual needs to stop "going to that place."

The solutions will differ. But one thing for sure, a well-examined Analysis will reveal real answers.

Now, write your Analysis in the Worksheet section on Page 88. After you finish it, write your Conclusion on Page 92. Identify your solutions in your Conclusion.

Issues In The Heart

Part V: WORKSHEETS

Issues In The Heart

Issue

Issues In The Heart

Rule of Law

Issues In The Heart

Facts

Issues In The Heart

Analysis

Issues In The Heart

Conclusion

Issues In The Heart

Final Notes

Oh friend, the Bible is the Rule of Law. It is the truth, and its words are alive today. The truth is that God's Word is good news.

Isaiah 26:3 states: God will keep him in perfect peace whose mind is stayed on him, because they trust him. I am a witness that this is true. No matter what is going on around you or how difficult life may be, God will keep you in perfect peace.

Psalm 27:14 encourages us to wait on the Lord and be of good courage, and he shall strengthen our hearts. Again, I am a witness that this is true. Do not get in a hurry and do things your way. God will meet you where you are. Wait on Him.

God's Word is true.

Absolutely!

The answer is in the Word of God. He wants to help you with any issue that you have. It does not matter what it is, how big your problem seems to be. God has a Word for your circumstance. It is the law, and your issue must surrender to it.

Give God a chance. Let Him help you.

Thank you for reading, "*Issues In The Heart*." I look forward to hearing from you and hearing your story, how God has repaired your lives and brought you to wholeness never to go back again.

Leave your thought on my Face book page at Lucinda Jones (Detroit). Visit my website at advocatelucinda.org.

Best to you!